A Lucky Story

A Lucky Story

Copyright ©2024 by David A. Green.
You can contact the author at me@davidgreen.run

ISBN 9798987321010 (Paperback)

All rights reserved. No part of this book may be used or reproduced in any manner whatsoever without written permission from the author, except in the case of brief quotations embodied in critical articles and reviews.

I have a magical story to tell you . . .

Once Upon a Time, in a faraway place, outside a little village in the mountains, I woke up to the sounds and smells of humans. While I never had a human friend, I walked the streets every day being friendly to others. If you saw me on the street, you would see a scruffy dog with thick black and brown hair, neither small nor large. Even though you'd see big sharp teeth, I am the friendliest dog you will ever meet. My left ear is perfect, my right ear is folded down. And, people think I don't smell very good because I've never had a bath.

In my village there are a few streets, some cobblestone and some dirt, but my favorite spot is the park right in the center. Although this park is loved by many, the town around it can be a dangerous place — either you belong to a gang of dogs with a strong leader to protect you or you are a loner like me. These gangs are fiercely protective of their posse and aggressive toward outsiders, so I am always on alert. This is why there is no better place to live than the park full of humans who sometimes give me food and even pat me!

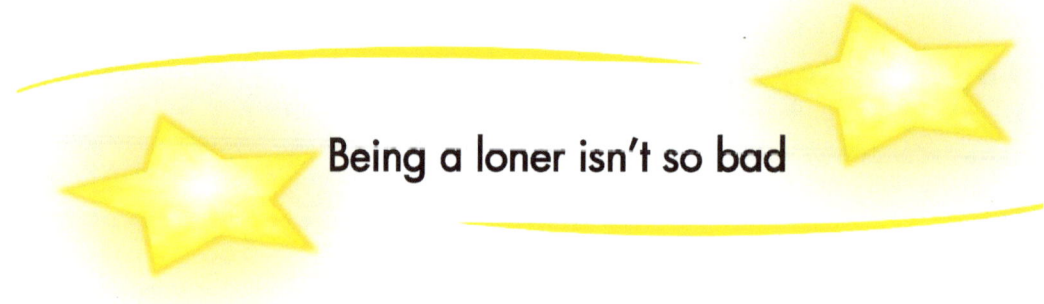

Being a loner isn't so bad

One day a group of humans ran into my village. And, they came right through the park! These humans were of all colors and smells. I love humans and love running so I decided that I would follow and see where they would go. I chose one group that smelled familiar and ran with them. I must admit I was a bit nervous as my familiar park faded into the distance, but the excitement and mystery of what lay ahead drew me forward. We arrived at a new village and I was happy because it had a park. I didn't know there were other parks in other villages and I began to wonder, what else could be out there?

Get out of your comfort zone and explore the world

Some time later, another group of runners came by, and they smelled very different. I was so curious that I acted on instinct and followed this new group on the trail out of town. On the way, we encountered a gang of mean dogs. One of the runners yelled at them and they backed down. I was nervous about the gang so I ran as fast as I could to catch up but as I neared them, the pack attacked — biting me on my neck and ear. I was determined to get by so I put my head down, ran with all my might, and did not stop until I was back with my pack of humans. They began calling me "Rover," which I learned means wanderer.

Trust your instincts and never give up

The humans began to share water and food with me.

And I decided that I liked them, liked running and exploring the world, so why not keep going!

Do what you love and follow your heart

That evening, one of the runners was limping and I was worried he would stop. He went into an ambulance while the others kept going. We were right next to the village park, so I was happy to wait for my limping friend. Later, as the sun went down, he came out of the ambulance and, feeling better, he left the village running into the mountains. I watched him leave but I wasn't sure if I should follow him until I realized that I already missed him so I decided to follow his scent. I ran hard on the trail, up a mountain, then down and finally at midnight, I found him sitting in a chair and I felt relief and excitement to see my friend again. I was very, very happy.

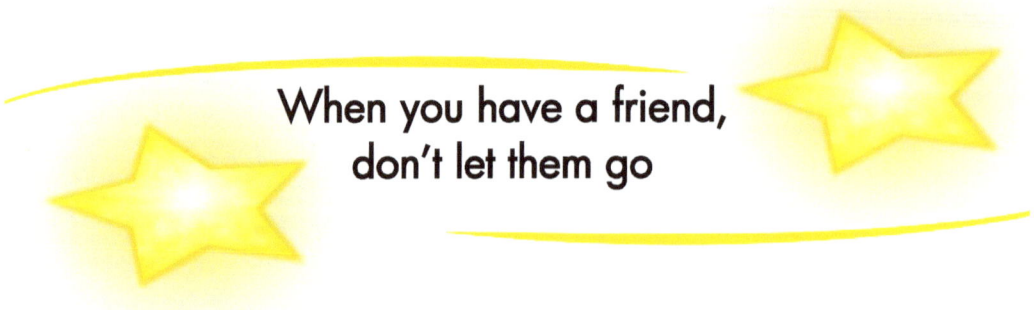

When you have a friend, don't let them go

Over a day and night, we ran through many villages, until we came across a small pousada or hotel. I had never been in a pousada or a house and was scared until one of the runners picked me up and carried me into a room; it was cozy and warm.

He put me in a bathtub, turned on the water, and washed me for the first time in my life — I thought I smelled funny because I have never used shampoo before! Afterward, I was super tired but so happy that I had found a friend who took care of me. Feeling clean for the first time in my life, I slept deeply.

Happiness is being cared for

Every child knows that dogs can talk to humans. But when humans get older it becomes harder for them to understand each other unless the dog is a "dogmate," just the way two humans who are meant for each other are called "soulmates." I had listened to the runners call my friend "David" — his name! His friends were Amy, Alan, Nivaldo, Bob, and Will. The next day we ran through a paradise of banana trees, red-clay trails, cool breezes, and friendly, familiar animals like cows and sheep. I thought I would try to speak to David and said, "Rover is a good name but I am not wandering anymore. I found you. And, I feel so lucky. Why not call me Lucky?" To my surprise, he heard me! And since humans have last names, he decided to give me the last name of Caminho, which means trail; after all, that is where we met.

Magic is all around us

Later that day we arrived at a village plaza where there were lots of humans cheering and giving out medals for anyone who crossed the line. Even I, Lucky Caminho, received a medal, and all the humans patted me, gave me food, and welcomed me to their pack like one of their own!

David could hear me, understand me, and take care of me; now I knew we would be dogmates forever.

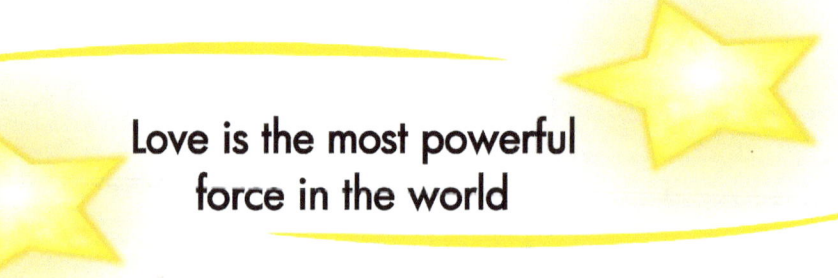

Love is the most powerful force in the world

The next day, a big mountain stood in front of us and we needed to cross it. On the streets, I did not have a lot of food and after so many days of running I was not feeling well. I told David that I needed to rest so he put me in the car and I was taken to a doctor in the next village. I listened as the doctor said, "Lucky Caminho can be healed. David, do you want to take him home with you?" And I heard his emphatic answer, "Yes! But I will need help getting him to a faraway place. . . ."

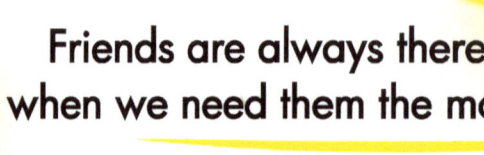

Friends are always there when we need them the most

A lot of human friends helped — a woman doctor healed me, a man took me and put me in a little house called a "crate," a woman drove me to the airport and then they carried me into the bottom of a giant airplane. I was a little frightened all alone high up in the sky without my best friend, so I decided to close my eyes, think positive thoughts . . . and then I fell asleep. I woke up when the plane landed and another man put my crate on a dolly and rolled me into a big hangar. I could not see David, my dogmate, but I could smell him from far away and I could not help but cry out in happiness because I knew my instinct was right and we would be together forever.

Believe and trust in those you love

I went to my new home and learned that I would have a baby brother and sister as well as an older, wiser brother that were just like me, adopted.

A family welcomes everyone

David and I ran every day. We ran long runs that lasted all day and sometimes we ran short runs. We ran around the neighborhood, and we ran in faraway places. I played with new animals — squirrels, raccoons, ducks, turtles, geese, frogs, and salamanders. And, I never wore a collar or a leash when we ran because I understood from David that I needed to be safe on the road, so I always stayed right behind him. I was so excited to run every day that I would wait beside his bed for my best friend to wake up each and every morning.

Play a lot and always be safe

And then one day, I said to David, "I do not feel well, I am tired." We went to a doctor who told us that it was something called "cancer" and that I did not have a long time to be with David. Now if you only had a certain amount of time, what would you do? I had lived on the street with no food, family, or home. I felt very happy and so lucky that I had met my dogmate and found a home. So I told David, "Let's do what we love to do. Let's go on the longest run ever, together." And it was decided that we would run across the big country of America! I saw new animals — big cows, deer with antlers, antelopes, rattlesnakes, bears, elks, eagles, and I even heard coyotes. I ran up mountains, jumped into rivers, and even chased antelopes across the prairies.

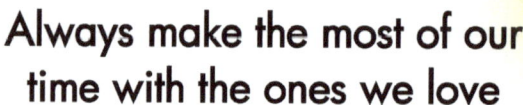

Always make the most of our time with the ones we love

Doctors helped me feel better and were surprised that I was running so far even though I was sick. They did not know that what was most important to me was that I was with David each and every minute of every day. We lived as if it were a dream, leaving nothing for tomorrow. And then one day when David asked me if I wanted to run that morning, I barked "yes!" as I always did. But as we went out together to start running, my body could not go on. I looked into David's eyes and told him, "We met on the trail and we have played together every day since then, it is time for me to go to sleep and for you to keep running forward. Even though you will not see me, I will be by your side forever as I have always been."

We will never lose the ones we love

You see, everyone will sleep peacefully one day — humans and animals alike, which is why it is so important to appreciate every moment with the ones we love. And when they are gone, every special memory we have of them will live in our hearts, forever.

And David knows this because the next morning he woke up and even though Lucky wasn't there, David said, "Lucky, do you want to run?" and the memory barked "YES!"

"Don't cry because it's over,
smile because it happened."
Dr. Seuss

Lucky in his park

Lucky meets new friends

Lucky's path is blocked

Lucky is given water and food

Lucky finds David on a mountain after losing him

Lucky stays in a pousada for the first time

Lucky is happy with Amy and David

Lucky finishes the ultramarathon and is awarded a medal

Lucky is very tired

Lucky arrives in the United States

Lucky arrives home and meets his brothers and sister

Lucky running in his new home with David

Lucky running across the United States of America

Lucky saying goodbye

Lucky will always be at David's side

Lucky & David ran 13,000 miles together over 44 months

A very special Thank You to

Amy　Alan　Nivaldo  Bob

Will Mario

Chris Alex　Gabriel

and especially

My partner Monica

In Loving Memory of "Great Grammy" Clea Meyers
104 years young

www.ingramcontent.com/pod-product-compliance
Lightning Source LLC
Chambersburg PA
CBHW041534040426
42446CB00002B/81